MUST-WIN DEALS

Must-Win Deals

How to Close Them

(and why we lose them)

Steve Thompson

VALUE LIFECYCLE™

MUST-WIN DEALS

How To Close Them (And Why We Lose Them)

ISBN   978-1-5445-1247-1 *Paperback*
         978-1-5445-1248-8 *Ebook*

Contents

Prologue

Approximately half of my work involves coaching and consulting with procurement specialists, purchasing managers, and senior executives with some of the largest companies in the world. In these engagements, I help them position and negotiate better and more strategic deals with their key suppliers. Working with these organizations, I have jointly developed a simple but powerful framework that represents the customer's view of an ideal journey—one that results in a mutually beneficial, long-term business relationship. As a result, my viewpoint encompasses more than just the sales side, and I want to bring a different perspective to help you see what is happening on the other side of the table.

The rapid growth and popularity of SaaS and subscription business models has suddenly shone a bright light on the need for "outcome-based" selling. It could be argued that customers have always wanted to buy new and (hopefully) better outcomes, only to be frustrated when salespeople focused on their products and services, making the buying decision much harder than it should be. For legacy salespeople and organizations, the challenges with implementing outcome-based selling are much greater than just uncovering the customer's desired outcomes. It also entails "connecting the dots" between those outcomes and key elements of your offering, proposing outcomes (versus products and services), negotiating on outcomes (versus just price), and finally delivering the promised outcomes after the sale. As you can see, it is much more than the "selling" that needs to change—which is why so many sales organizations find pursuing outcome-based selling so challenging. This is the essence of the concepts I will share with you in this book and throughout the *Must-Win Deals* series.

To be clear, the *Must-Win Deals* series is not a sales process. Nor is it a negotiation or account management process. Instead, it follows and explores an overarching framework that focuses on the critical customer touchpoints and outputs of your *existing* processes. These are the essential tasks that, if well executed, can supercharge your current practices and systems and make it far more likely that you will land "must-win" deals, keep key customers, and grow your business with them.

As for my buying clients, their response to the series can be summed up as *Where have you been?* and *What do you think we've been saying all these years?*

Foreword

"Your price is too high," said the procurement manager with a tone of finality. "In fact, your competition is more than 20 percent cheaper, and we'll be awarding the business to them. I'm sorry, but the decision has been made, and it is final."

Wait, what just happened? For ten years this has been one of your company's biggest and most reliable accounts— one you were sure you couldn't lose. You were expecting a routine annual renewal *and* an upsell. Worse, your boss was expecting the *increased* bookings from this marquee account to hit her number for the quarter. Now you've got to explain, both at work and at home, how you just lost your biggest commission check of the year—and your shot at the President's Club!

If this scenario feels at all close to home, this book is for you. If you're a sales leader concerned with quarterly quotas that too often ride on a handful of key accounts, this book is for you. For sales managers and sales professionals who make their living in the B2B world—people who find, position, propose, negotiate, and close critical deals with other businesses—this book and the other books in the *Must-Win Deals* series provide pragmatic, straightforward guidance for more than just closing must-win deals. They're about retaining and growing sustainable business following the steps in the Value Lifecycle™, a seller's framework built around the customer's buying journey (detailed in chapter 2).

It all starts with a clear-eyed look at the challenges we too-often put in front of the very businesses we're trying to sell to—the ones that make it harder, not easier, for them to *choose us*. This turn of phrase is key, as it speaks to a shift in perspective that will inform the rest of the series. Throughout, we'll be looking at the selling process from the customer's point of view as a way to both understand *and change* the way we think about selling.

WHY FOCUS ON MUST-WIN DEALS?

Must-win deals are must-win for a lot of reasons. You could be working a large deal that's getting outsize attention from senior management, with big political blowback if you lose. Or a significant new marketplace may be on tap if you can close an influential gateway customer. Maybe you're a "land and expand" SaaS business, which makes every deal that much more strategic—if you land on the *right deal*. Or it could just be that final deal that gets you to your annual quota. However you define them, must-win deals are usually complex, long-term, high-stakes engagements with huge political and strategic importance to both sales professionals, their company, *and* the customer.

Now ask yourself a question: *Can you afford to take on critical sales challenges like these by doing more of the same things—or is it time to consider doing something different?*

Here's a little "news" to help you decide: If you've been reading from the same sales playbook year after year, you should know that your customers—and your competitors—have only grown more sophisticated. You can argue that the fundamentals of selling (and buying) are the same as they've always been, but you can't ignore the impact of the internet and other disruptive technologies on the selling ecosystem, even in the B2B world. Buyers have access to more options, sellers have more access to potential buyers, and many supply chains have evolved in some markets to make even the need for selling questionable. The result is that your customers can scare up a price war and set off a "race to the bottom" more effectively than ever before, and there will almost always be someone more desperate who can "run" that race faster than you!

In this context, the reason for focusing on must-win deals should be starkly evident—and urgent. After all, the other side of a complex sale is a *complex purchase*, and there are often multiple players on each side and multiple items on the table. Beyond a product or service, there's volume and discounting, close date, terms and conditions, ancillary services, and follow-up support. In short, complex deals are expensive, time consuming, and often painful for *both sides*. This makes price-only negotiations all the more frustrating and illogical, as they set the stage for the next "deal," which will again be all about price.

I submit that the only cure for this *rinse-and-repeat* madness is one of the most critical and overlooked aspects of B2B selling—an ongoing, sustainable business relationship. The word *sustainable* has received a lot of attention lately, and for good reason. In walks of life from civic to environmental, we're beginning to appreciate the value of systems that, once established, require minimal inputs to keep running, or perhaps even grow. Business is no different, and the ongoing value of a sustainable business relationship is becoming more of a driver for how we *should be* selling, negotiating, and managing accounts after the sale. What's more, the goal of a sustainable relationship must inform how we manage our business.

Still, in the prevailing, quarter-driven business environment, sustainability is the first casualty of short-term thinking, and the outcomes for business are sometimes disastrous. Consider these examples:

→ Depending on industry and study, it costs from five to twenty-five times more to land a new customer versus keeping an existing customer. (*Harvard Business Review*, 2014)

→ *Bain and Company* reports that a 5 percent improvement in customer retention will increase profits by 25 percent to 95 percent! (*Harvard Business Review*, 2014)

→ According to *Invesp*, 44 percent of companies focus primarily on new customer acquisitions, while only 18 percent focus heavily on customer retention. (*Econsultancy*, 2013)

→ The probability of selling to a new prospect is only 5 percent to 20 percent. The probability of selling to an existing customer is 60 percent to 70 percent. (*MarketingMetrics*, 2016)

→ For SaaS businesses, it costs $1.13 on average to acquire $1.00 of ACV from a new customer—only $0.13 to retain $1.00 of ACV from renewal. (*Pacific Crest*, 2016)

The value of ongoing, sustainable business relationships is clear, and the goal of this series is to show how we should go about cultivating them at the beginning of the sale—with new *and* existing customers.

In *Must-Win Deals*, I will show you how, as sellers, we make it unnecessarily challenging for customers to award us any deal—much less a large or critical one. For only by understanding the challenges we present to customers can we learn how to remove or reduce those challenges, dramatically increasing our odds of winning, and winning big! The remaining books in the *Must-Win Deals* series will address in more detail how we overcome and manage each of these challenges.

But first things first. What are these challenges we present to customers?

This book is the first in the five-part *Must-Win Deals* series. The second book, *The Irresistible Value Proposition*, reveals the technique behind a value proposition that makes customers want what you're selling—and want it now! The third book, *The Compelling Proposal*, showcases the proposal as a strategic tool to reinforce trust and credibility, making it easy for the customer to choose you (and trust their choice), and manage the uncertainty inherent in the real world. *The Painless Negotiation* then explores capturing the value in not just any deal, but a great deal for you and your customer. The final title, *Can't-Lose Accounts*, delves into delivering the promised value, which makes renewals simple, referrals enthusiastic, and upselling and cross-selling much easier. I hope you will derive great value from this journey!

CHAPTER 1

Why We Lose

We Make It Challenging for Customers to Award Us the Deal!

When I work with selling clients, I often poll the salesforce and ask them for the number one reason they lose deals.

"The price is too high," is the typical (and expected) answer.

"So when you win deals," I respond, "it must be because you have the lowest price, right?"

"No. We win because we sell the value!"

There's something telling about this exchange. In terms of what you control, you win deals because the customer sees the value of your offer—and the size and speed of closure is directly related to how much value they see. In terms of what you control, you lose deals because the *customer does not see the value.* It's that simple.

But simple is not the same as easy.

Many of the factors that cause you to lose (or slip) must-win deals are completely beyond your control. A key buying influencer has suddenly left the company, significantly delaying a decision. The customer is acquired by a larger company and all projects and initiatives are put on hold. Last quarter's financial results were pretty ugly, and budgets are frozen until senior management can sort out what needs to be done. These are events you can't control, so there is no reason to spend time on them. (They do point up an important caveat, however: always maintain more sales pipeline than quota!)

It is much more productive to focus on things you *can* control, like the four key challenges you inadvertently present to potential customers—the ones that make it challenging for them to *award* must-win deals to you:

1. Your customer ***doesn't understand your value proposition.***
2. Your customer ***can't connect their value goal with your proposal or offer.***
3. Your customer says ***your price is too high, and you***

don't have a negotiation plan to keep the value in the deal.

4. Your *existing* customer ***doesn't know the past value you've delivered.***

It shouldn't surprise you that each of these challenges is tied to value. Although it is one of the most abused and poorly understood concepts in business, value is (and always will be) the real currency of B2B selling. So it's worth restating and anchoring on this simple concept: You win deals because the customer sees the value in doing business with you. When they don't (or can't) see that value, it's usually because you've presented one or more of these four challenges. So let's explore them in a little more detail. After all, when you get them right, you can dramatically increase your odds of winning—and winning big.

*Your customer **doesn't understand your value proposition.***

Your value proposition should be what makes your customer sit up, take notice of what you are saying, want what you are selling—and want it now. But this can only happen if your customer clearly understands your value proposition, and it is relevant to the outcomes they wish to achieve.

Let's start by clarifying the *type* of value proposition we are talking about.

Many salespeople confuse the more general *marketing* value proposition with the targeted *sales* version, which is specific to the customer and their situation. A (simplified) marketing value proposition might go like this: "We save customers money." Its primary purpose is to generate sufficient interest from a prospective customer to get them to check out your company and your offerings. As such, it is rarely enough to generate a sale. (By the way, it is likely a marketing value proposition that your competitors are using in their sales process.)

A *sales* value proposition more directly addresses the customer's specific situation and what they want to accomplish. It might state, "We will save you money," then specify *what* money, *how much*, and *by when*. Your job is to make your value proposition clear, irresistible, and specific to your customer so that they want what you're selling and want it sooner rather than later.

You could argue that this type of value proposition is the logical output of any sales process, and I wouldn't disagree with you. But as an *output* it has no value. Don't leave it to your customer to deduce your value at the *end* of the selling cycle. Rather, get out in front with a value proposition that answers the questions your buyer is going to need answers for. Don't make them work for it!

The next book in this series looks at the sales value proposition in detail.

*Your customer **can't connect their value goal with your
proposal or offer**.*

When I work with buying organizations to help them
position and close critical deals with key suppliers, part
of my job is to review supplier proposals. I almost feel
bad getting paid for this work because I already know
what almost every supplier proposal will say. They're all
about the suppliers and their products, services, features
(sometimes benefits), office locations, growth, recent
acquisitions, etc. They're all innovative, world-leading,
and Gartner upper-right quadrant. And I don't know
how this math works, but somehow they all manage to
be number one in their field. It's no wonder customers
have a hard time choosing one supplier over another and
often end up making the safest and most logical choice:
the vendor with the lowest price.

In short, the current state of supplier proposals is truly
abysmal. And they stay that way because many sales
reps simply cut and paste from previous proposals and
templates. (With any luck, they also remember to search/
replace the customer name!) The other problem is that
these proposals are constructed more like marketing
documents than ones meant to close a sale. The more

pages—pictures, diagrams, charts, graphs, tables—the better. They then become self-defeating, making it harder for the customer to make an informed decision because nowhere are these mountains of data linked to the outcomes the customer wants to achieve. As a result, customers begin to question why certain elements are in the proposal. Are these vendors "padding" their bid? Do they really understand our business and what we want to accomplish?

The form of a proposal should follow its function and objectives. Its function is to seamlessly and quickly bridge from selling to setting up the right negotiation. Its objectives are to (1) reinforce trust and credibility, (2) make it easy for the customer to choose you (and feel confident they have made the right choice), and (3) manage the uncertainty that surrounds any complex deal in the real world.

> In the third book in this series, we will introduce a simple seven-page proposal that will be compelling to the customer, accomplish all three objectives, and more.

*Your customer says **your price is too high, and you don't have a negotiation plan** to keep the value in the deal.*

It should not surprise you when customers tell you that your price is too high, that the competition is cheaper, or that they only have so much budget. (These are all basically the same thing.) Yet most salespeople are not prepared to deal with these predictable objections—especially when made by buyers in must-win deals. Instead, sellers run back to the "mothership" and beg for a bigger discount or try to throw in some services for "free," moves that both delay the decision and devalue the deal.

In short, they are negotiating the wrong way.

And blinded by eleventh-hour nerves, what most sellers can't see is how customers read these theatrics. At some point, your buyer will begin to question the value of what you are trying to sell them. You told them your products are world-class, so why are you so quick to give them away? If they were as good as you say, you'd stick to your guns. I've seen a deal go off the rails because the customer got so uncomfortable with the seller's panicked "negotiation" style, they just cancelled the deal. The supplier was negotiating the wrong way and, as a result, the customer's *perceived* risk was too high.

What many salespeople also fail to consider is that a deal won primarily on price will affect every future deal with that customer. What you readily give away or concede today will be the *starting point* of the next negotiation in the next deal. Worse than that, customers talk to each other. People change jobs and companies, and they remember the previous deal they did with you. In this way your negotiation style spreads, helps to establish the true market positioning of your company, and can broadly impact future business.

Remember, your goal when negotiating is to keep the hard-earned value that you created in the deal, resulting in a great deal for *both parties*.

In the fourth book in the *Must-Win Deals* series, we explore the topic of negotiating—ensuring that we are having the *right negotiation* and that we are negotiating the *right way*. The fifth and final book in the series covers the concept of past value delivered.

Your *existing* customer **doesn't know the past value you've delivered**.

I know, I know—you're worried about landing that must-win deal *right now*, and you're not thinking about when the value is delivered after the sale. Odds are, in your organization what happens after the sale may not even be your responsibility.

This thinking works—until it doesn't.

Let's assume you're trying to sell a big deal into an existing account, a long-standing customer. If that customer doesn't understand the past value your firm has delivered, why would they be interested in buying more from you this time (maybe a lot more)? This single issue gets in the way of closing must-win deals more times than I can count. When a customer knows they've received *some* value but aren't sure what it was, their default assumption will usually be that they paid too much for it, and a tough, price-only negotiation is bound to ensue. This is the "teachable moment" for most sales reps, when their organization's failure to focus on past value delivered comes into sharp focus. It's a shame because the easiest sale in the world is to an existing, happy, *informed* customer.

Your customers already have enough challenges making complex, high-stakes buying decisions, and the last thing they need from you is even more hurdles to clear. So why not give them a straight and clear path when dealing with you: Be sure your value proposition is easy to understand and that your proposal clearly connects your offering to the outcomes they are trying to achieve. Anticipate price challenges and have a plan to counter with options based on *value*, not discounts. And finally, be sure they understand the value you have delivered in the past so that they are not focused on finding the next lowest bidder, but on *value beyond price* in their ongoing relationship with you.

* * *

If you haven't figured it out by now, this book (and the

entire *Must-Win Deals* series) is built around the idea that successful selling—the kind that closes big, strategic deals and leads to ongoing relationships—can only happen in a context of mutual value. That is, value to you and to your customer. Of course, that means that we're going to explore in some depth what value means to your company, but what about your customer? How in the world do you go about determining what value means to them?

It starts by appreciating and understanding the context of value within your customer's "buying journey."

CHAPTER 2

Your Customer's View of the Journey

It's the Value, Stupid!

As previously mentioned, about half of the work I do is on the buying side, coaching and consulting with some of the largest companies in the world. Over the years, I have helped these organizations position and negotiate better and more strategic deals with their key suppliers, and it may surprise you that the top priority for these buying organizations—second only to getting a fair deal—is establishing (or growing) sustainable and mutually beneficial business relationships with the organizations they buy from. More simply put, they are looking for both short- and long-term value.

What this work taught me, as I compiled and compared

notes on both sides of the table, is that the buying process follows a predictable pattern—a cycle—that, ideally, builds on the value created from previous engagements. It also taught me that buyers, not sellers, were the main drivers of this process. The reason for this is simple: *they are the ones spending the money*, often millions of dollars at a time! Naturally, their strategic focus is on getting the most value from every engagement and converting and growing that value by building relationships with critical vendors.

In the end, what really surprised me was how much more intuitive the buyers' understanding of this strategic buying cycle was than the sellers'. Time after time, I have worked with selling organizations, often very large ones, that simply did not grasp the strategic buying focus of their target customers. This was true even when they were selling to *existing* customers. Clearly the need existed for a framework to help guide these sellers and give them a "map" of the customer's ideal buying journey.

That is why I created the Value Lifecycle™, a "buyer's journey" with three straightforward phases, *Create Value*, *Capture Value*, and *Deliver Value*.

THE VALUE LIFECYCLE™ IN BUSINESS RELATIONSHIPS

Figure 2.1: The Value Lifecycle™

The Value Lifecycle™ informs how we should sell, how we should negotiate, and how we should manage accounts after the sale. As you can see, there's no clear beginning or entry point, and no end point, as each stage of the cycle derives from the previous one while driving the next. At the core (or "heart") lives the simple, immutable goal of every company: win customers, keep them, and grow more business with them. This is to drive home the fact that, no matter where you are in the Value Lifecycle™, both acquisition *and* retention share equal importance in how you should think about creating sustainable (vs. transactional) value with your customers.

I have found that companies that are world-class at executing the Value Lifecycle™ framework enjoy some fairly powerful benefits:

→ They have much less account churn.

→ They enjoy higher conversion rates when selling to new customers.

→ They have higher margins on the deals they close.

→ Their sales cycles are shorter.

→ They benefit from higher success rates at cross-selling and upselling.

→ They retain customers longer.

In many cases these companies are virtually bulletproof from competitor attacks—nobody is going to take that account away from them!

Let's take a quick walk around the Value Lifecycle™ to understand in a little more detail how successful sellers map their sales motion to the customer's buying journey.

THE VALUE LIFECYCLE™ STEP 1: *CREATE VALUE*

When I work with B2B salespeople, I am always interested in their response to the question "What is selling?" Now keep in mind that this is what they do for a living, but if I have twenty to thirty salespeople in the room (from the same company), invariably I get twenty to thirty different responses. Think about that. They make a living selling—every day—but their descriptions of what they are being paid to do are all over the map.

So, is it safe to assume that if most salespeople have different definitions of selling, odds are they aren't doing it equally well?

THE VALUE LIFECYCLE™ IN BUSINESS RELATIONSHIPS
CREATE VALUE

Figure 2.2: Create Value

Let's start with the overall objectives of any business, and the heart of the Value Lifecycle™: to win customers, keep them, and grow more business with them. Remember, the Value Lifecycle™ is a seller's tool built around the customer's buying journey, so it makes sense to look at these objectives from the customer's perspective. When you are selling, the customer wants you to *create the potential for value*, both for them and for their business (Figure 2.2). Whether you are selling a product or service (or both), it's just that simple. But let's not confuse *simple* with *easy*. Selling into a B2B environment can be complex and drawn-out. Solutions are getting more sophisticated, and the number of buying influencers on the customer side is increasing. But what you are trying to accomplish is straightforward: *creating the potential for value* for that customer.

To that end, B2B selling can be simplified and summarized as follows:

→ **Solve meaningful problems (or capitalize on meaningful opportunities)** on or before the desired due dates.

→ **Sell to the right people** who own and have a priority to achieve the desired outcomes against their success metrics.

→ **Understand the alternative you are up against.** Ensure that you can provide more value than the alternative, and that you have a strategy for beating that alternative.

→ **Present an irresistible value proposition** that compels the customer to want to close the deal quickly.

→ **Determine all of the customer's buying steps** and where the money will come from, so that you can manage the steps and target a realistic close date.

Although B2B sales cycles are usually long-term, iterative processes—after all, how often does a customer take your initial offer?—successfully executing on these five fundamentals will almost certainly "create value" and lead to a business negotiation.

THE VALUE LIFECYCLE™ STEP 2: *CAPTURE VALUE*

Sales organizations tell me that they are negotiating all the time and that it is critical to their success. But when I ask what negotiating is and what "negotiating all of the time" really means, I get yet another twenty to thirty different answers. Again, as with defining "selling," if a sales organization lacks a consistent and clear definition of negotiating, what are the odds they are effectively (and consistently) executing their negotiations?

Negotiating is nothing more than *capturing the value you created when selling in a great deal for both you and your customer.*

THE VALUE LIFECYCLE™ IN BUSINESS RELATIONSHIPS
CAPTURE VALUE

Figure 2.3: Capture Value

Let's look at your hypothetical progress as a seller up to this point. You uncovered an opportunity and successfully sold it. You negotiated a deal and obtained a purchase order. Walking down the cubicles in your regional office, you get high fives and fist bumps from your associates. You exceeded your quota and, of course, received a commission check. Things couldn't be much better, and life as a salesperson is good—really good!

But how do things look from the buying side?

A bit different. The customer had the "pleasure" of multiple meetings with not just you, but your competitors' salespeople too. They listened to all the pitches, although they likely lost track of which pitch came from which vendor. Then they had to turn around and sell their idea up the corporate food chain to justify a potential spend on the project. Some organizations would have further required them to go out for bid with an RFP, which meant writing the RFP (a painful, iterative process), then submitting it to a list of potential suppliers, including you. The buying organization then had to read through the proposals submitted by the suppliers. After the customer read all the proposals, they selected you and then likely had to justify their selection within their organization.

If you have never read one of your proposals, I encourage you to do so. And try to read it through the customer's eyes. You will probably find the exercise somewhere between boring and mind-numbing. In all likelihood, the proposal is all about you, the seller, not about them, the buyer. Is your current proposal format making it easier to choose you and your company? We'll spend an entire book on this topic alone.

At this point, the customer is scared to death. They have made a commitment—to you, the supplier, and to their senior management. They face serious political blowback if it doesn't go well, not to mention significant business implications. Their confidence is about as low as it can be in the overall relationship. So why in the world, with all this pain, process, risk, and uncertainty on the buying side, are you on the selling side having a party? Because what we sellers call "the show," buyers view as an achingly slow, sometimes boring, and often painful prelude to what they consider the main event.

What the customer really wants is for you to *deliver that value you promised!* What's more—and this is key—they actually want to give you credit for it. Now if you have been in sales for any length of time, you may be a little jaded on this point. Why would your customer want to give you credit for delivering on something you promised and got paid for? The answer is simple: because *they chose you*, and when you deliver the promised value, they look smart for choosing you.

THE VALUE LIFECYCLE™ STEP 3: *DELIVER VALUE*

How does delivering value and getting credit for it benefit you as a salesperson? For starters, you can expect painless renewals, eager referrals, and new opportunities to upsell and cross-sell within that organization. Show that you can create value and negotiate a deal that is good for both sides, ensuring that all the key elements are there to allow both parties to deliver the value. Then deliver—or over-deliver—on that value. Do these things, and your customer will give you credit and go to bat for you both inside and outside the company. This is where a lot of new sales pipeline should come from. It is always easier to sell to a *current, happy* customer.

THE VALUE LIFECYCLE™ IN BUSINESS RELATIONSHIPS

Figure 2.4: Deliver Value

Aside from time, the biggest challenge with getting credit for past value delivered is that most salespeople have little experience doing it. That's understandable because selling organizations tend to lack the processes and cadence to regularly meet with customer key decision makers after the sale. But this time should be prioritized, and customer value review meetings should be considered as important as any other step in the sales cycle. It's like fertilizing a garden. You won't see results that day, and maybe not even for a week or more, but eventually the results of your effort will bear fruit—bigger, better, and juicier ones at that.

Beyond confirming PVD, another key benefit of regular customer value reviews is the increased value you will be able to bring to future meetings, when the customer is considering new business challenges to address or opportunities to pursue. You may be invited into such meetings earlier in the sales cycle because of the interest you showed in ensuring that the last solution you brought was returning the expected value. Much of this work after the sale is not immediately about dollar signs, but the competitive advantage you can gain by ensuring PVD can make all the difference when new opportunities arise. In short, ensuring and getting credit for past value delivered is one of your most important tools in developing a mutually sustainable business relationship that is based on value.

If your business is *something* as a service (SaaS), then the Value Lifecycle™ is even more critical to your success. (For the record, SaaS, to me, is *any* subscription service, as so many subscription models are based on a delivery framework similar to software.)

THE VALUE GOES ON AND ON

Now that we've completed a high-level tour of the Value Lifecycle™, note that it has no clear beginning or end. If you want to keep a customer for a long time, you must confirm that you have delivered value in the past, and when you uncover new opportunities, ensure that you are creating the potential for new value with that customer. When negotiating, make sure you are capturing that value in a deal that is *good for both sides*—then you are back to delivering value and receiving credit. It goes on and on. This is how your customers view an ideal, ongoing business relationship with trusted suppliers.

THE VALUE LIFECYCLE™ IN BUSINESS RELATIONSHIPS
ONGOING VALUE

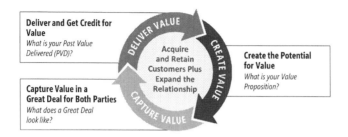

Deliver and Get Credit for Value
What is your Past Value Delivered (PVD)?

Capture Value in a Great Deal for Both Parties
What does a Great Deal look like?

Acquire and Retain Customers Plus Expand the Relationship

Create the Potential for Value
What is your Value Proposition?

Figure 2.5: The Value Lifecycle™

If "selling" is starting to feel like a four-letter word to you, you're in luck. And I'm guessing you've already figured out the issue: you are *selling*, but what is your *customer* really doing?

CHAPTER 3

What Are You Selling?

More to the Point, What Are Your Customers Buying?

Much has been written about the changes and challenges in the world of B2B selling, and there is sure to be more disruption ahead. But our aim is not to repeat what you probably already know or to try to predict the future. Instead, I offer a single, general observation. No matter what information and insights technology may facilitate, a search engine can never provide the answer to the most important question a customer asks when making a buying decision: *Who really understands me, my problems, and what I'm trying to accomplish?*

There is no doubt that B2B selling is getting more challenging. Reps often complain that the sale is just getting too complex. There are too many buying influencers on the buying side (and often too many "helpers" on our side). And things keep changing at a seemingly faster pace—leading to even more uncertainty and risk. What most salespeople don't appreciate is how much the risk and uncertainty are magnified on the buyer's side. After all, they're the ones committing to spend often huge sums of money. As a result, our job is to mitigate risk, minimize uncertainty, and make it easier for the customer to make the right decision.

That is why I submit that there will always be a need for talented salespeople—especially those adept at creating value for their customers and communicating that value effectively. And since the way organizations think about value is directly influenced by how they think about buying, let's look at how we should be thinking about selling, through the customer's lens.

As illustrated in Figure 3.1, the first step in a customer's buying process is to identify a business opportunity they want to pursue or business problems they want to solve. I have found that organizations spend much more money pursuing business opportunities, like launching a new product or executing a new go-to-market strategy, than solving current problems. But in either case, companies are prepared to commit resources to achieve an outcome, or future state, that is different from their current state. In other words, they are really buying a *result* or *outcome*—not a product or service.

ACHIEVING OUTCOMES (CREATING VALUE WHEN SELLING)
How Customers Typically Think about Buying

Figure 3.1: Achieving Outcomes

If the outcome has high strategic or business value, a company often implements initiatives with defined objectives. Someone (or perhaps a team or committee) is made responsible for achieving the outcome. Priorities are established by the buying organization because there is rarely sufficient budget to address every possible problem or opportunity. (If it is not a high-priority outcome, then it is probably not worth pursuing as a seller.)

At some point the key decision maker, or group, also develops success metrics, which they will use to measure value (more on this in *The Irresistible Value Proposition*, the next book in the series). It's worth noting that these metrics typically coincide with how the team or key decision makers are measured. As a result, the issues that get attention are typically the ones that impact promotions, pay raises, stock options, etc. At this point, the company is ready to explore and evaluate alternatives. This may take the form of a stringent, formal process such as an RFI or RFP (or both). Finally, the buyer chooses a solution and negotiates a deal.

The "shape" of this process is an inverted pyramid because at the very beginning, when customers first contemplate what they want to accomplish, things are generally big-picture and perhaps a little vague. As the customer moves through their buying journey, clarity grows, and the conversation becomes more focused and granular as *who*, *what*, *where*, *when*, and *how much* are answered, until the final deal is negotiated.

Looking at this model, sales teams tend to sell one of two ways: reactive or proactive.

REACTIVE SELLING

An opportunity is only real when it has a "budget" behind it—when the buyer is already halfway through their buying process and is at the point of evaluating alternatives and issuing RFPs.

Right?

Judging from the behavior of many (if not most) sales organizations, the answer is *yes*.

Here's the problem with that thinking: At this stage the customer has already decided what they are going to do—and they've decided that *without your influence or input*. If it is a formal buying process, they may have handed you an RFP, and you are simply responding to specifications or requirements. Not only did you not help develop those requirements, there's a good chance that a competitor (or consultant) did. And whoever that was, you can be sure of two things: (1) they had an agenda, and (2) it didn't include you and your company. At this point you—and many of your competitors—are just "bid fodder."

This is *reactive* selling, where suppliers' value propositions usually distill down to a feature/function/price beauty contest. In my experience, companies that wait until this stage in the customer's buying process have win rates in the single digits. What's worse, if your company clears the minimum feature/function hurdle, as some of your competitors are likely to do, then the deal will probably come down to a price-only "negotiation."

Bottom line, if you've been trained to engage buyers only when there is a "funded project and they have a budget," then you are *bringing very little value* to the table, and you will be evaluated against similarly "qualified" competitors. Reactive deals like this are hardly a recipe for creating long-term, mutual value.

PROACTIVE SELLING (GENERATING DEMAND)

But what if you engage the customer much earlier in their buying process, when they are trying to get their arms around the potential outcomes their company could achieve and the business problems they could solve? This is when you can help shape the conversation, define the opportunity, and, ultimately, the deal. Your value proposition is now focused on *business and personal* value for the customer rather than *technical* value. As a result, not only will your deals grow in size, but your sales cycles should shorten, and you'll engage in much less bickering over pricing and discounting.

It's worth stressing that these deals make much more economic sense for both you *and* your customer, not least because they are often sole-source and not even taken out for bid. Time, after all, is money.

ACHIEVING OUTCOMES (CREATING VALUE WHEN SELLING)

How Customers Typically Think about Buying

Figure 3.2: Creating Value When Selling

If you're going to *create the potential for value* for your customer, the ideal time to do so is in the early stages of their thinking (Figure 3.2), when they are trying to address their business opportunities and problems. You create significant value when you help them think through what they could do, the potential outcomes available to them, and what they should focus on, not to mention potential pitfalls to avoid. How do I know this? Most of my buying clients initially engage me to help them negotiate better deals with suppliers, but I invariably spend most of my time helping them think through the initial steps of their buying process before we can begin to address the negotiation issues. In short, we work together to ensure that they understand (1) the outcomes they want to produce and are ready to pay for, (2) the right solutions for those outcomes, and then (3) the right negotiation.

This may sting a bit, but odds are your customers don't wake up every day thinking about you, your company, or what you sell. No one says, "Life would be great if I could just buy more widgets from Sarah!" So if that's the case, what are you selling? Can you answer with more than a list of products or services? Now ask the question a different way, from the customer's perspective, "What are we buying from Sarah, and why are we buying it?" Ultimately, isn't *this* what you are selling, and wouldn't it be great to have insight as to *why they might prefer to buy it from you*? For example, while Sarah thinks she's selling widgets, the customer may look at Sarah's real value as *saving them time* (and therefore money) because Sarah's selling process is more focused on their outcomes than her competitors.

As the top of the pyramid shows, what customers *buy*—and what you should be offering—are solutions to business problems, or solutions that allow them to pursue business opportunities. In short, they are buying desirable outcomes. But sales organizations tend to be so taken with (and trained continuously on) their own products or services that they can't see the outcomes their customers are trying to achieve. This internal focus is misguided and costly because while customers may *pay for* products and services, what they are *buying* are different outcomes. They are looking for a future state where things are better than today. And the way the customer measures the success of these outcomes is the way they will ultimately measure value.

WATCH YOUR LANGUAGE!

If you want customers to recognize the value you are offering, then you should state that value in their language—not yours. If they fail to understand your value because you haven't explained it to them in *their* language, using their metrics, odds are they won't be interested in buying it.

A profound marketing analogy from Theodore Levitt of Harvard drives this point home.

"People don't want to buy a quarter-inch drill. They want a quarter-inch hole."

PROFESSOR THEODORE LEVITT, HARVARD UNIVERSITY

When you go to the hardware store and purchase a cordless drill and a box of bits, what are you really buying? When you think about it, you are *buying* holes (the outcomes), though what you are clearly *paying for* are a drill and drill bits, the tools that facilitate the goal of holes. Some of the features on that drill may be critical to producing the types of holes you want. For instance, a cordless drill will enable you to drill holes virtually anywhere. But is the battery powerful enough to drill through something stronger than wood and durable enough to drill lots of holes? Do you need a backup battery and charger? Do you have the right assortment of drill bits? These features are relevant because they relate to the holes (outcomes) you want to produce.

Keeping with the analogy, your customers are measuring the value of your "drill" in terms of how quickly, inexpensively, and consistently they can produce the quantity and quality of "holes" they want. If you sell a service, then things become even more nuanced. When selling a service to a customer, they are basically subcontracting the production of holes to your company, in which case it is even more crucial that you understand the exact outcomes (holes) they are looking for. Think about this if you are in a SaaS business or rely on a subscription model.

Now that we've established that customers are buying outcomes, we need to tie those outcomes to the right bundle of products, services, support, volumes, etc. that they will pay for in the deal we sign. But instead of just aiming for any deal that we might be able to close, we should be aiming for the *right* deal structure that will result in a *great deal for both of us.*

CHAPTER 4

Aiming for a Great Deal

Why Not Hit the Bullseye?

Jack has just been unofficially awarded a very large deal by his customer's operations team, a deal he's been working on for the past six months. This single deal will put him into accelerators and give him and his wife a trip to Club! All that remains is to complete the negotiation with a very tough procurement manager, but he needs to get it done this week to meet his quarter *and* year-end quota. To make matters worse, senior management expects this deal to be closed as it has already been factored into the guidance given to Wall Street. This certainly qualifies as a "must-win" deal.

No pressure, Jack.

This morning, the procurement manager told Jack that there was no hope for closing this deal within the week because his discounting was "way out of line" with the competition. When Jack pressed him for numbers, he said the discounting was at least 30 percent too low. Now Jack was in a panic! If he discounted that much more (if his management would even approve it), he would not exceed quota, meaning no accelerators and no Club! So Jack hustled back to headquarters and presented his case to sales management and finance for more discounting, though it felt more like begging. Finally, after much gnashing of teeth and pulling of hair, he got them to agree to a steep additional 20 percent discount. After all, what choice did they have?

At a meeting the next afternoon, Jack proudly presented the additional discount to the procurement manager, who calmly looked him in the eye and said, "Good start, Jack. Now let's talk about the cost of implementation services and training. We expect you to include these items in the base price, just like your competition. And if this isn't resolved quickly, we'll be forced to seriously reconsider a competitor's offer."

The sick feeling in Jack's gut was now beyond panic. Services and training made up over 15 percent of the total price of his offer. If he gave those away, he'd never meet quota. He put in a quick call to headquarters as this decision would require not only sales management and finance, but also the VP of operations. As he sped back to the office for what promised to be an even tougher internal negotiation, Jack wondered where the customer's operations team (the end user) was in all of this—and how his world had so suddenly turned into such a mess.

* * *

What just happened here? How did this six-month engagement, which Jack had put so much energy and thought into, so quickly devolve into a price-only negotiation with a procurement manager?

Odds are, Jack didn't sell to critical customer outcomes, and on their own, the customer didn't make the connection between the various elements of his offer and those outcomes. That's why procurement was "out for blood" and feeling so empowered to negotiate with him. To say the least, Jack and his company were not ready for this negotiation. And even if he had given some relief on the implementation services and training, the procurement manager was just getting warmed up! The next demand would have been for better payment terms or some other spiff. Every time Jack was rushing back to the "mothership" for permission to give something else away, procurement was just having fun.

This is a "death of a thousand cuts," where no single cut is fatal, but by the final deal you're bleeding to death. In the end, what Jack "negotiated" was a terrible deal for him—and most likely his customer too.

I see this situation all too often and can usually trace it back to two root causes. First, the seller doesn't know what a great deal looks like, so they are not aiming at a clear target. (Their customer also doesn't know, because the seller did not educate them.) Second, they are not prepared to negotiate and to manage the tactics they expect procurement to use, and they become completely isolated from the real customer, which in Jack's case was the operations team.

We'll address negotiation in the third book in this series. For now, let's explore this concept of a *great deal* that leads to the *right deal*.

DEAL LEVERS: THE ELEMENTS OF ACHIEVABLE OUTCOMES

We've established that customers are buying outcomes, and that you should be selling *to* those outcomes. But it's important to emphasize that you don't actually sell outcomes. In fact, you *can't* sell an outcome. What you sell are the products and services, bundled into a business deal that will produce those outcomes. Figure 4.1 shows typical business and personal outcomes in B2B deals.

EXAMPLES OF OUTCOMES

Business Value	Personal Value
∗ Increase revenues	∗ Meet goals and objectives (MBOs / KPIs)
∗ Lower costs	∗ Commission, bonus, pay raise, promotions
∗ Process improvement	∗ Receive personal and team recognition
∗ Increase customer satisfaction	∗ Improve relationships
∗ Reduce risk, Corporate Image	∗ Reduce political risk

We Achieve These Outcomes by Putting in Our Offer(s)...
Those *Deal Levers* that support the **business and personal outcomes**
each side is trying to achieve

Figure 4.1: Examples of Outcomes

I call these bundled elements *deal levers*. A typical way we start outlining the specific deal levers for an opportunity is to first identify the *products and services* that should be included in the deal. But that only makes up a small portion of the deal levers. We need to also think about:

→ The appropriate *contractual* elements of the deal (such as liabilities, warranties and guarantees)
→ The *business* transaction (volumes, discounts, payment terms, close date, etc.) items that are important
→ The *strategic* items that could help us get more business with this customer or other customers (customer value reviews, executive access, references, referrals, etc.)

These are just a few examples. A more detailed thought-starter list is provided in Table 4.1 and the Appendix. Note that this list is generic by necessity, as it applies to most businesses in B2B sales. Different businesses and industries have their own nuances and peculiarities that result in special items being incorporated into deals, which must be taken into account. This customized list is something my clients pay me to create so that they can more effectively execute their sales and corporate strategy. The value to you should be clear: thoughtfully and thoroughly answering these questions will help you build a detailed list of deal levers that you can use to construct a better deal for both you and your customer.

DEAL LEVERS – EXAMPLES
Converting Outcomes Into Key Elements of a Deal

1 Solution Levers	2 Contractual Levers	3 Business Transaction Levers	4 Strategic Levers
◾ Product #1 ◾ Product #2 ◾ Service #1 ◾ Service #2 ◾ Etc.	**Which Contract** ◾ Master Agreement ◾ Addendum ◾ SOW ◾ Purchase Agreement **Key Contract Terms** ◾ Liability & Indemnification ◾ Service Level Agreements (SLA) ◾ Warranties ◾ Guarantees ◾ Cancellation Provisions	◾ Discount ◾ Volume ◾ Future Price Increases ◾ Date of Close ◾ Schedule / Completion Dates ◾ Contract Term ◾ Payment Terms ◾ Level of Support ◾ Training ◾ Travel Expenses	◾ Reference Account ◾ Co-Publish and Present Papers ◾ Joint Engagement Planning ◾ Customer Value Reviews (Who and When) ◾ Influence Technology Roadmap ◾ Introduction to Other Departments / Divisions

Table 4.1: Deal Levers – Examples

Remember that one of the challenges your customers will have in awarding you a critical deal is that they can't easily connect the elements of your proposal—the *deal levers* in the offer bundle—to the outcomes they are trying to achieve. Your task is to first determine the deal levers that should be in a deal based on the outcomes both your customer *and* your company want to achieve. Then educate the customer on the right deal levers in your value proposal. (We'll cover the outcome-based proposal in book three of the *Must-Win Deals* series.) Figure 4.2 illustrates how this might be done.

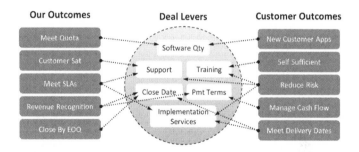

CONNECTING THE DOTS – OUTCOMES & DEAL LEVERS
Transforming Outcomes into Key Deal Elements

Our Outcomes	Deal Levers	Customer Outcomes
Meet Quota	Software Qty	New Customer Apps
Customer Sat	Support Training	Self Sufficient
Meet SLAs	Close Date Pmt Terms	Reduce Risk
Revenue Recognition	Implementation Services	Manage Cash Flow
Close By EOQ		Meet Delivery Dates

Figure 4.2: Outcomes & Deal Levers

Let's focus first on "connecting the dots" to the customer outcomes in this example. The customer wants to launch new apps for their customers. Therefore, the quantity of your software solution should correspond to producing that outcome. The customer also wants to become self-sufficient, so naturally, staff training should be in the deal. If the customer is concerned about the risk of this initiative, then support after the sale and implementation services should also be in the deal. Payment terms are also important to help the customer better manage cash flow. Finally, to meet the committed delivery dates, the "close date" of the deal and implementation support should be included. (Note that linking the close date to customer-required delivery dates is often missed when selling, and then everyone is surprised when deals slip. Make the close date the *customer's date* too.)

As the seller in this example, you want to meet quota, so the quantity of software you sell is important. You want a satisfied customer after the sale, and you know this often correlates to the support level purchased. To meet certain service level agreements, you also want to do the implementation and have the right support level after the sale. Your finance department cares about revenue recognition, so you care about payment terms. Finally, you need this deal by the end of the quarter to meet quota, so naturally you care deeply about the close date.

The point is that a deal can only be a *great deal* if it works for both you and your customer. The logic here is fairly simple: if a deal is not good for one side or the other, it doesn't matter how much money was made or saved during the negotiation; if the right outcomes are not achieved, it could threaten the ongoing business relationship. This is why it is critical that you approach must-win deals with a solid, thoughtful list of deal levers. Think of them as the negotiation currency of shared value. There will probably be deal levers that both sides want in the deal. These will provide a solid foundation for mutual value in the deal. Other deal levers will provide more "give and take" at the table, and the best way to sort out which is which and how best to deploy these elements is to define early in the sales cycle what a great deal looks like for you and your customer.

DEFINING A GREAT DEAL

To ensure that you're going to make the *right sale* and then have the *right negotiation*, you must start with an understanding of what a great deal looks like in your particular situation—not just the target you're aiming for, but the *center* of that target. This, as we will see, is the only way to know what you will be prepared to accept. I've seen salespeople who lack this understanding take just about anything (especially those with insufficient sales pipeline). They are "shooting blindfolded," and a lot of them shoot themselves in the foot!

A great deal has three attributes:

→ High value to the customer as it meets their buying objectives and supports their desired outcomes
→ High value to the seller as it meets their sales objec-

tives and supports their long-term strategy for the customer
→ Key deal levers that allow both sides to ultimately *deliver the value*

Now, although we are still early in the sales cycle, I want you to assume that a deal *is going to happen* and ask yourself, *what does a great deal look like?* This is the first of three key value questions that you must consider (see the sidebar). Answering this question will begin to reveal some critical insights into the opportunity you are beginning to pursue, including:

→ The compelling deal levers that both sides want in the deal (joint value)
→ The deal levers where both sides are potentially far apart
→ What each side might be willing to trade to address those differences (negotiation plan)

Your job is to determine which deal levers create joint value and are least likely to be an issue when negotiating. You should also identify the levers where each side may be far apart. The earlier in the sales cycle you understand these things, the more time you will have to bridge gaps and find other deal levers that each side may be willing to trade to overcome any differences. This makes a huge difference when the formal negotiation begins.

THREE KEY VALUE QUESTIONS

1. Based on outcomes important to each side, which deal levers would constitute a *great deal* if we were to reach agreement? (This Book)

2. Based on desired outcomes, what are the impacts of the *most likely alternative* (MLA) each side must accept if there is no agreement? (Next Book)

3. Based on desired outcomes, what *anchors* must we manage, and how should we anchor? (Fourth Book)

Now let's take a step back and revisit an important tenet in outcome-based B2B selling: *you neither sell nor negotiate outcomes.* What *the customer pays for* are bundles of deal levers (solutions) that enable your company and your customer to achieve those outcomes. Why is this concept so important? Because it will keep you focused on finding the right deal levers that will ultimately make up the best possible deal—for both sides—and therefore facilitate a successful negotiation.

SET YOUR PRIORITIES AND KNOW YOUR LIMITS!

You've just completed the first step in defining a great deal: understanding the deal levers you'll need to achieve the customer's outcomes while supporting your sales and business strategies. So what does a great deal look like? Figure 4.3 provides a template for determining a great deal. (See the Case Story in chapter 5 for a detailed example.)

Based on the Outcomes each side is trying to achieve, determine a Great Deal:

* List of Deal Levers
* Ranking or Priority
* Limit (Ask For – Accept)

Levers	Limits
1. _____	(Ask – Accept)
2. _____	(Ask – Accept)
3. _____	(Ask – Accept)
4. _____	(Ask – Accept)
5. _____	(Ask – Accept)
6. _____	(Ask – Accept)

Figure 4.3: Determining a Great Deal

Then, because not every lever holds the same importance in a given deal, you should prioritize those deal levers. Start by considering higher-priority levers that must stay in the deal for you to achieve your sales goal. Then determine the lower-priority levers you could trade away to obtain something of greater importance. This is precisely how most successful business deals are negotiated, and if you have not carefully considered all of the levers in the deal and prioritized them, you will not be prepared to trade effectively.

Finally, world-class organizations sit down internally and define clear upper and lower *limits* (ranges) for each item. For example:

→ We will offer a 15.2 percent discount, but if pressed we're prepared to give up to a 20.4 percent discount.

→ We will ask for an initial order of 1,000 units, but if the customer objects we will take a minimum volume of 700.

→ We'd like to close by August 31, but if the client delays, we will honor the remaining portions of the deal only until September 30.

Sit down with your internal stakeholders as early in the sales cycle as possible and determine the limits on all of your deal levers. You can always revise terms and numbers as the deal evolves and new information becomes available. This is the heart of your *internal negotiation*—sorting out what you and your company really want (or need) and what you're willing to accept. By looking at the whole deal, everyone involved understands what it means to your company, and everyone can get on board with the target. When you allow your internal stakeholders to see what you are trying to achieve and what it will mean to the business, you will find that most are much more willing to "give" on something they own. After all, most sales management and internal stakeholders are good corporate citizens who are willing to take a minor hit in their area of responsibility to help you land a deal that is good for the business.

If you do not conduct your internal negotiation this way, it will almost certainly conflict with the external negotiation with the customer. Just remember Jack, whose internal negotiation was conducted in a state of panic at the end of the sales cycle—something I see all too often.

What's more, world-class organizations will empower their sales reps to negotiate any deal as long as it's within their internally agreed limits. No more harried flights back to HQ for permission. This can significantly compress the time needed to negotiate and close deals, which is good for the sales rep, the business, and the customer. Furthermore, it can significantly drive up the quality of those deals. Defining what a great deal looks like ahead of time gives everyone a clear view of the target you are trying to hit. Defining the deal levers and limits prepares the selling organization to have the "right negotiation."

In my experience, roughly 75 percent of the time, selling organizations do not understand what a great deal looks like to them. As a result, they are *almost always* caught out in negotiations. They just don't know what they are prepared to accept and are therefore not ready to negotiate. This is good for my business, but bad for theirs!

WHAT ABOUT THE BUYER?

Since every sale and negotiation process involves two parties, let's look at the same question with regard to buying organizations. How often does the buyer go into a potential purchase and negotiation with a clear understanding of what a great deal looks like to them? Perhaps surprisingly, not that often.

About 90 percent of the time, based on the outcomes they are trying to accomplish, the buying organizations I work with do not understand what a great deal looks like to them. It's important to keep in mind that buying organizations are not necessarily experts at what they buy. And aside from the increased strategic focus that spending large sums of cash tends to bring to the group writing the check, should we really expect the customer to be any more aligned internally than we are?

Now if about three out of four sellers and nine out of ten buyers don't understand what a great deal looks like to them, logic suggests that most deals being closed are *not that great*. So how much value could you bring to your company if you worked with your internal stakeholders early in the sales cycle defining that great deal for your organization? And what if that work enabled you to then help your customers define their great deal when they were in the early stages of their buying process? In a competitive situation where you are helping a prospective buyer define the "target," you are going to be *ideally situated to hit that target*. Still, this simple, logical strategy—early internal negotiation followed by external consultation—is one that sales organizations miss time and again.

Once you've done your internal "homework" and you understand the outcomes your customer is trying to achieve, you are in a position to help them understand the levers of a great deal: the ideal blend of solutions that will give them the highest probability of achieving their outcomes. Which services. What level of support. What type of payment terms. What sort of volume discounting or pricing. When the deal needs to close to hit their desired commitment dates.

Just remember that all of this should happen as early as possible in the buying process (Figure 4.4), when the customer is trying to identify where to focus, where they're trying to go, and the best way to get there. Then both you and your customer will understand the target you *are both* trying to hit in the sale and subsequent negotiation.

We'll discuss the internal and external negotiation in greater detail in books three and four of the Must-Win Deals series.

ACHIEVING OUTCOMES (CREATING VALUE WHEN SELLING)
How Customers Typically Think about Buying

Figure 4.4: Achieving Outcomes

This wraps up the key concepts for *Must-Win Deals*. To help bring it all to life, I've created a case study in story form—a *case story*, which will continue throughout the *Must-Win Deals* series to demonstrate how all of the concepts are linked in the Value Lifecycle™. While the story is fiction, the characters are based on very real archetypes, and the events are derived from my numerous experiences in client engagements over the years. Any resemblance to actual events or persons is purely coincidental, of course, but no one could blame you if it sounds familiar. After all, I've seen similar scenarios unfold so many times—there might as well be a script.

CHAPTER 5

Case Story

Paul Stockard is a sales rep for **Agile Information Solutions (Agile)**, a one-billion-dollar provider of cutting-edge software and storage as a service (SaaS) solutions. Through their advanced cloud-based infrastructure, Agile enables customers to more efficiently manage data storage, and their software provides access to customers' critical databases and applications. For the past five months, Paul has been managing a key existing customer, **Worldwide Financial Solutions, Inc. (Worldwide)**, and he has been working on what should have been a routine three-year renewal. However, it was just announced that a much larger company is acquiring Worldwide, and the renewal has been put on hold while Agile learns more about what the acquisition will mean for Worldwide. Paul was recently promoted from small accounts, and despite this development—or maybe because of it—he really needs to show sales management that they made the right decision and that he has what it takes to bring in sizable new deals.

One of the defining characteristics of Agile's technology is that it allows customers to eliminate much of the technical infrastructure needed to store and access their critical data. This reduces the cost of hardware, software, and staff while allowing companies to focus on what they do best. It also allows businesses to more quickly expand infrastructures and configure new applications as they grow and evolve.

Because of the explosion of digital data generated by customers, Agile has grown by leaps and bounds in the past ten years and now enjoys a strong reputation for high-quality solutions combined with expert implementation services, all backed by excellent support after the sale. After all, the data Paul's company helps its customers store, manage, and access is often the lifeblood of those businesses. What's more, Agile's solution is designed to easily scale as their customers grow.

Agile is a big player in the small and medium business (SMB) space, with 55 percent of the market pie, fully 35 percent more than their next closest competitor. Recently, they have begun to win some business with Fortune 500 companies, resulting in deal sizes many times larger than those with their SMB customers, not to mention much bigger commission checks. Naturally, this is where Agile's executives see the company growing, and it looks like Paul may have stumbled into one of these opportunities.

Worldwide, easily the largest of Paul's accounts, provides a full range of investing services to businesses and high-net-worth individuals. With Agile's support, the company has developed an award-winning web portal and mobile application that have helped drive both growth and strong customer satisfaction. Worldwide has grown its business significantly with Agile for eight years as it has acquired smaller companies and merged with competitors, and Agile's solutions have been instrumental to its growth strategy. Now Worldwide's success has drawn the attention of major Wall Street players, and it is in the process of being acquired by **Mega Financial Services (MFS)**, one of the largest financial services businesses in the world. According to the press releases, MFS covets the high margins and high growth of Worldwide and its offerings—areas where MFS is strategically weak—and the company has a very large customer base to sell these services to.

Three weeks ago, when the acquisition was announced, it was the talk of Wall Street. The consensus of financial analysts was that Worldwide's innovative products and services would be a huge boon to MFS and represent a significant competitive advantage if they could be offered to new MFS clients. In addition, Worldwide would create significant short-term revenue growth if its services could be rolled out to existing MFS clients. But Paul and Agile are now on the outside looking in, and Paul is very worried about his three-year Worldwide renewal, as it represents a significant portion of his quota, and he assumed it would be a lock.

* * *

Susan Renly is the chief information officer at Worldwide. She is Paul's day-to-day contact, and over time Paul has come to view her as an ally. Paul and Susan have been working closely together for almost six months since Paul took over the Worldwide account, and they have a cordial, mutually supportive relationship. A week ago, Susan reached out to Paul to fill him in on the acquisition. Paul had been trying to reach her since the news broke, so he was happy to take her call. She asked him to come to her Worldwide office in the afternoon to discuss what the acquisition might mean for Agile as well as to her and her team. Paul was understandably nervous, but he needed to get a handle on the situation—and fast!

At her office, Paul greeted Susan warmly, but uncharacteristically they skipped their customary small talk and got right down to business.

"Paul, this MFS acquisition has thrown a monkey wrench

into everything we've planned. I'm sorry I have not been able to return your calls, but I do want to fill you in on what I've learned from all the meetings I've attended over the past couple of weeks. I think you'll find some of this very interesting."

"I'm all ears," Paul replied, feeling a knot forming in his stomach.

"For starters," she began, "you need to know that **Kenneth Beckley**, my boss and the soon to be ex-CEO of Worldwide, has been named to the board of MFS. He has also been charged with ensuring that our mobile apps and customer portal are converted to MFS platforms and that the MFS salesforce uses these moving forward."

Paul shifted uncomfortably. He didn't see how this had any positive bearing on his renewal, which was all he was focused on at the moment.

"As far as I'm concerned," Susan said, speaking directly to Paul's discomfort, "Agile is the supplier of choice. But you should also know that you'll be seeing some stiff competition from **JCN**. They're the incumbent technology infrastructure provider at MFS."

With that, in spite of Susan's assurances, Paul's hope for a renewal vanished, and the knot in his gut grew tighter.

"Surprise!" Susan exclaimed ironically. "I bet you came in here just wondering how the acquisition affected your renewal."

Paul gathered his wits. Susan was being direct but supportive—and not a little bit coy—which helped him get past the raw emotion. "Well, now that you mention it," he said, "I was kind of wondering where we stood with the renewal. But I'm really confused. What's this about Agile seeing stiff competition from JCN?"

"Paul, let me reassure you," she said. "The renewal was just approved by Kenneth this morning. He doesn't want anything to get in the way of the integration. I think it was about a million and a half, right?"

"Yes," he responded, visibly relieved but still trying to master his emotions. "The invoice was $1.48 million. And you're saying it's approved?"

"You'll see the signed contract in several days and payment within thirty," Susan smiled. "But I think you're missing the point here. The renewal is *small potatoes* compared to what I'm talking about. This opportunity is probably ten times larger!"

"Whoa!" Paul exclaimed, genuinely shocked. "I like the sound of that. But Susan, walk me through this—slowly.

How can Agile be in competition with JCN? Worldwide was just bought by MFS, right?"

"Okay, okay, here's the big plot reveal," she laughed. "Paul, you know I wouldn't have strung you along if this was all bad news! Kenneth was tasked with ensuring that the MFS salesforce has complete access to Worldwide's applications and data. Now, I can tell you that most MFS executives just assumed that we would convert all of our data and applications from your cloud infrastructure over to the MFS on-premise infrastructure supplied by JCN. However, in a meeting this morning with other board members and the MFS CEO, Kenneth questioned the wisdom of that approach, and he managed to convince them that they should at least explore a cloud-based solution as an alternative, like the one we use today at Worldwide. In other words, there's a chance we will actually *move the MFS data and applications over to Worldwide's cloud infrastructure—provided by Agile, of course!*"

She paused briefly and watched Paul's face as he took in the information.

"Now do you see what I'm getting at?" she asked. "And while you're thinking about your answer, I want you to know that this also represents a huge opportunity for me. If we pull this off, I have a real shot at the CIO position at MFS, so naturally I want to help out any way I can."

"Okay, got it," Paul said plainly, finally recovered from his shock and newly anchored by Susan's clear-eyed support of him and his company. "Thank you!"

"Don't thank me yet," she chuckled. "The political winds are swirling around this deal, and we need to keep a sharp eye on the weather vanes. I'm not the only one with a big stake in the outcome!"

Paul laughed. "To say I didn't expect this is the understatement of the decade! So what do you need from me?"

Susan laid out her request, the real reason for this meeting with Paul. She admitted that she was not adept at positioning a deal as large as this, especially with all of the politics surrounding it. However, she was confident that Paul and Agile could scope the situation and come up with the best approach for Worldwide and MFS. To be sure, they would have to move fast, as things were progressing quickly. They agreed to update each other the next day.

On his way back to Agile, Paul phoned **Tim Rosser**, his VP of Sales, to fill him in on the news. Tim was pleased with the renewal, of course, but he was uncharacteristically silent after Paul told him about the new scenario Susan had relayed concerning the Worldwide acquisition.

After what seemed like a long pause, a smile crept onto Tim's face.

"Well, Paul," he exclaimed, "congratulations and welcome to the big leagues!" He reminded Paul that now there would be no room for error, and this potential opportunity would have visibility all the way to the executive suite at Agile. What's more, this single deal would exceed Paul's quota for the entire year and get him and his spouse a ticket to Club.

After his chat with Tim, Paul wasn't sure if he felt better or worse. There was so much potential, but so much work—and so much he still didn't know! He called the account team and asked them to meet with him in an hour. At this stage of the sale, every minute was critical, and they needed to work out the very real problems that Agile would be solving for MFS, and the opportunities they might be creating for them. They also needed to put together an outline of a great deal for Agile and MFS. According to Susan, they were now in the land of very large deals, and they would need to be well equipped to master the terrain.

Back in the meeting room, Paul briefed the team.

"The technical challenge is fairly straightforward," he began. "MFS needs to access the databases and applications of Worldwide, and neither party is using the same platform or hardware. Now we all know that this kind of project is Agile's bread and butter, and right in our wheelhouse, but this appears to be a much bigger integration than we've ever pulled off. What's more—and this is key—we still don't know the business problems or outcomes that are important to MFS."

Paul and the account team spent the day researching the history of MFS and the latest press releases and analyst reports concerning the merger, and it emerged that the business problems were most likely revenue growth and customer turnover. Prior to the announced acquisition, MFS had been losing twice as many customers as their competitors, with customers apparently opting for smaller, more innovative providers with investment options much like those offered by Worldwide. What's more, sales growth had slowed at MFS for three quarters, and their once high-flying stock was languishing. During the past few days, the CEO of MFS had been quite vocal in assuring Wall Street that the company had an answer for this issue.

While some at Agile viewed this as strictly an IT opportunity, Paul and most of his team felt that MFS saw it as a revenue and customer retention issue. As such, the key decision makers would more likely be in the C-suite than in IT, although both audiences would have to be taken into account. In other words, this was an issue for the entire business, so Paul's first challenge was to identify the key buying influencers at MFS.

This was a problem, as Agile had never worked with MFS, and Paul had no contacts there. But he did have Susan Renly. As a key supplier, Paul and his predecessor had held regular customer value reviews with senior management at Worldwide, where he had developed strong relationships, including Susan. She had just confirmed her strong support of Paul and Agile in their earlier meeting, and her position and reputation, both within Worldwide and now with MFS, could be pivotal in giving Paul and his team the access they needed. Paul and Susan had already booked a follow-up call, and the agenda was now a lot deeper!

The next day, Paul called Susan as planned, and they quickly got down to business.

"Paul, this situation is getting richer by the minute," she laughed. "I've been chosen to co-lead a steering committee that will oversee the integration of Worldwide into MFS. They wanted me because of Worldwide's proven experience integrating acquisitions. And it's worth noting that this is an area where MFS is very green."

"My fate is in your hands," Paul joked, though he was genuinely thrilled by the news.

"Maybe," she said, "but now that some of the political dust has settled, it turns out that one of the reasons I was chosen is that the CIO of MFS recently resigned. His position is being temporarily filled by the current VP of Technology at MFS, and unless you drank the stupid juice this morning, you'll surmise that I'm now officially in line for formal promotion to the CIO position."

"I had coffee," Paul quipped back, "and it's telling me that we need to work together to make sure you get that promotion."

"Let's give it our best shot," she said, "starting with a technical briefing. How soon can you and your technical team come to MFS to present an overview of your solution to the IT department? Yesterday would be good."

Paul chuckled wryly, and he and Susan agreed that if all went well with the presentation, Agile would then be asked to perform a technical proof of concept (POC) to demonstrate how their solution would perform in the MFS environment.

"Of course we'll be there," Paul confirmed, "and we'll be fully prepared. I really appreciate the invitation, but I have a few more questions, if I may."

"Fire away," she invited.

"I suspect that the real business issues for MFS are revenue growth and customer churn. And they view Worldwide as a possible solution to those issues. Am I aiming at the right target here?"

"You're on the dartboard," she confirmed.

"And will the steering committee have the final say in this decision or will other buying influencers be in the mix?"

"The steering committee is responsible for making the final recommendation," she clarified, "*and* implementing that solution."

Susan explained that the steering committee consisted of the VP of Technology, **Jack Grossman**, along with a senior procurement manager, **Stephanie Holder**, and the SVP of business operations at MFS, **Bill Sellers**. Paul took thorough notes as this was critical information for his team.

"I'm the 'outsider' on the committee," she laughed. "But the man who signs the checks is Bill. He has some real skin in the game, and he's under pressure to make this integration happen quickly."

"But Paul, listen," Susan added with some urgency, lowering her voice. "Confidentially, JCN is highly connected at MFS. This is one of their largest global accounts, and they'll do almost anything to keep Agile out." She explained that JCN was especially tight with Jack Grossman, the acting MFS CIO and presumed to be her primary competitor for the empty slot of CIO.

"Wow, I'm glad I asked!" Paul exclaimed. He was now confident that MFS's alternative to Agile was JCN, and at this point that alternative looked challenging. But the more important strategic issue was whether MFS would decide to import all of Worldwide's data and applications into their current on-premise infrastructure, which was supplied and supported by JCN, or if they would consider a cloud-based services solution from Agile. To get their heads around a possible answer, Paul and his team needed to understand the entire scope of the potential engagement and start to flesh out what a great deal might look like for Agile and MFS.

"I also need to know about the scope of moving the entire MFS infrastructure to our cloud platform," Paul continued. "There's a lot involved in this type of project, as you well know, and we need to get a handle on what that will entail. Who should we meet with to talk about scope?"

"I'm way ahead of you there!" she chuckled. "My team has been pulling that data together, and we should have it ready before you begin the POC. As you know, we've worked together enough on integrations, and we know exactly what you'll need to be successful."

"That's great, and I can't thank you enough for all of your help," Paul answered. "We really need to get our arms around what's involved here—and quickly—if we're going to have a shot. Please keep me informed of anything new you learn, and I'll do the same."

Susan and Paul agreed to speak on the phone at least once a day until this was over.

First things first, Paul thought as he hung up the phone.

Before engaging in any high-level strategy, he and the team needed to provide an objective demonstration of Agile's technology to the MFS IT organization. Luckily, this was a standard exercise and part of Agile's typical selling motion. He knew he could count on **Jane Jones**, his sales engineer, and **Doug Hand**, the lead engineer for Services and Support, to handle the demonstration. Of course, Paul would be present to ensure things went smoothly and to learn anything he could.

Several days later, as expected, Agile's technical presentation went flawlessly, and the proof of concept testing began in earnest as a member of Susan's team delivered a scoping document. *This thing is huge*, Paul thought as he thumbed through the reams of data. *Let's hope the opportunity is at least as big!*

Paul's phone chimed with some interesting news from Susan. She had just come from a high-level meeting with Bill Sellers. Bill had stressed that the successful integration of Worldwide databases and applications was priority number one; nothing else took precedence. In a meeting with the board of directors several days before, Bill had been "asked" to commit to a timeline of no more than four months to complete the integration—and the clock started that day! Apparently, recent drops in MFS share prices were driving the board to make this happen as soon as possible.

When Paul asked, Susan told him that she believed Bill was looking for three key outcomes. First, the MFS sales and account management organization needed complete access to Worldwide data and applications. Second, the implementation should take no longer than the four months dictated by the board. Third, the entire integration should be completed within budget. This information gave Paul a much clearer understanding of how MFS would measure success (and most likely how Bill Sellers would measure value). However, Susan wasn't able to give Paul an idea of the available budget, because the acquisition of Worldwide involved a lot more than the IT integration. There were significant costs associated with redundant facilities, personnel, etc. that also needed to be addressed, but she was not involved in these areas and couldn't speak to the costs directly.

Paul called the entire account team together and told them he wanted to scope this opportunity ASAP and begin the process of outlining what a great deal would look like for Agile and MFS. The account team consisted of Paul, Jane Jones, Doug Hand, and **Jared Carlisle**, the senior financial analyst. Wasting no time, Paul passed out copies of the scoping document from Susan's team and filled them in on the progress to date as well as what he knew from his conversations with Susan Renly.

"In short," Paul began, "we believe we know what MFS is trying to solve for, we're fairly confident we know what is important to Bill Sellers, the key decision maker, and our competition is JCN. Now we need to determine how big and complicated this opportunity is and what sort of deal we should be aiming at."

Paul then reminded the account team, "We're assuming that MFS will do a deal with Agile, and our job is to determine what a great deal might look like. There will be no 'aiming low' on this one." The team chuckled; they'd all been *there*. "Let's work on this until we've got something for me to present to management tomorrow. Doug and Jared, I'd like you to be at that meeting. Jane,

I know you'll be busy with the POC, so we'll try to get on without you."

At his previous company, Paul had learned to dread the internal negotiation, a series of "running gun battles" with internal stakeholders that always seemed to happen at the worst time possible—right at the end of the sales cycle while trying to close a deal. Too often this also coincided with the chaos and panic at the end of the quarter.

But Agile was more proactive and smarter about internal negotiations. Their senior management believed that meeting earlier in the sales cycle and calmly determining what a great deal looked like, then empowering the sales rep to negotiate the deal, gave them a real competitive edge and allowed deals to get negotiated and closed faster. What's more, Finance had analyzed the deals done with this approach and shown that they were, in fact, much more profitable. However, the pace and size of this MFS opportunity meant that determining a great deal had never been more important. The stakes were high for this MFS opportunity, and Paul had to be ready for some tough questions in his meeting with Agile senior management.

At 8:00 a.m. the next morning, Paul sat down with Tim Rosser, VP of Sales; Jared Carlisle, senior financial analyst; Doug Hand, lead engineer for Services and Support;

and **Caroline Borders,** Agile's VP of Legal. He spent the first half hour briefing Tim and Caroline on what had transpired to date, then fielded a few questions, and the meeting seemed to be going smoothly. On a pair of flipcharts, he summarized what his team had determined to be the important outcomes for MFS and Agile (Figure 5.1):

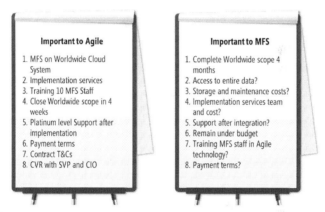

Figure 5.1: Important to Agile and MFS

"As you can see," Paul explained, "we have some pretty solid insights, but we have even more questions to answer."

Everyone agreed that, lacking direct confirmation from the key buying influencers at MFS, this was a pretty good place to start. Then Tim stated flatly, "Paul, I think it goes without saying that getting confirmation and filling in the missing information is job one for you and your team. I hope you've all cleared your calendars."

Paul laughed and assured them that his team was prepared to work around the clock to get confirmation on the outcomes important to MFS.

He then turned the group's attention to the next task, briefing them on what his team felt was the best "straw man" for a great deal with MFS. Everyone agreed with the list in general, and they spent the next hour finalizing the deal levers that would make a great deal for Agile and MFS, prioritizing those levers and then assigning preliminary limits for each. Many questions remained for some of the items, of course, but everyone agreed that this deal, summarized in Table 5.1, had the potential to be Agile's largest—ever.

GREAT DEAL FOR AGILE AND MFS

Priority	Levers	Limits
1.	WFSI Software Discount ~$14M	(30% Discount – 35% Discount)
2.	Implementation Services $920K	($950K – $800K)
3.	Training 10 MFS staff onsite $80K	($80K Onsite – $60K Offsite)
4.	Close Deal in 4 weeks	(2 weeks – 4 weeks / schedule slip)
5.	Platinum Support $240K	($250K - $125K / Gold Level)
6.	Payment Terms (Upfront)	(Upfront – ½ Upfront / ½ Completion)
7.	Case Study and References	(Case Study & Reference – Reference)
8.	CVR quarterly with SVP and CIO	(Quarterly – Semiannual)

Table 5.1: Great Deal for Agile and MFS

Paul left the meeting satisfied that they had done the best work they could do at this stage of the deal. He was exhausted but grateful to be working for a company with the foresight and discipline to get out ahead of such an important and potentially career-making opportunity by laying the groundwork for him to sell and negotiate with the full confidence of his senior management.

The prioritized list of eight deal levers and limits gave him exactly what he needed to go back to his team and prepare them for the sales campaign and, hopefully, negotiation.

1. Worldwide/MFS scope software and storage at approximately $14 million. With a list price of $20 million, Paul can offer a 30 percent discount (net $14 million) but can go as high as 35 percent discount (net $13 million) if the scope is strictly for Worldwide/MFS alone. Should the scope increase, such as for future acquisitions, Paul will be given more leeway, pending senior management approval.

2. Implementation services, to meet the aggressive MFS Board schedule, will require a lot of the top talent at Agile. Doug Hand, the lead engineer for Services and Support, can only estimate the price between $950,000 and $800,000 unless the timeline is also changed.

3. Experience has taught Agile that customers are

always happier with solutions when their staff are fully trained on the software. Agile has also seen that training is more effective and better attended when conducted at the customer's location. Therefore, training for ten MFS IT staff on-site will cost $80,000. Paul is authorized to go down to $60,000, but then the training must occur at Agile facilities.

4. Normally, the close date (especially before the end of the quarter) is important to Agile. However, this has been a very strong quarter to date, and Tim Rosser and Jared Carlisle are fine with the deal closing next quarter. They don't want Paul in a position where time is his greatest weakness in the sale and negotiation. However, if the close date drags on much past quarter end, then Agile will not commit to meeting the MFS Board deadline.

5. Experience has also taught Agile that support after the sale is key to customer satisfaction. Paul will offer the platinum support level, which includes a dedicated call-in number and dedicated team, for $240,000 per year, but if he is pressed hard on price, he can downgrade them to Gold Support for $125,000 per year.

6. Payment terms are pretty standard for the industry, and it is not unusual to ask for full, up-front payment. There was a time when this was important to Agile, but now that the business has grown, it is not as critical. As such, Paul will ask for up-front payment for software and storage for this deal. But with the addi-

tion of implementation services, he is authorized to accept one-half payment up front, with the final half upon completion.

7. A case study and a reference account could be very valuable to future sales, especially in the enterprise space. Paul will ask for a formal case study with references for six prospects, but Agile is prepared to accept references for only four prospects.

8. Agile has also learned that customer value reviews (CVRs) are essential for both getting credit for past value delivered and staying relevant with customers' current senior management. This is key in positioning new opportunities. Paul will ask for a CVR every quarter with the SVP of Operations and the new CIO, but he can accept a CVR with them just twice a year.

While nothing was cast in concrete, these deal levers put some structure around what a great deal might look like for Agile and MFS, and with preliminary limits in place, Paul and the team would be able to validate some key assumptions. Given the fast pace of this opportunity, these deal levers provided much-needed focus for the team moving forward.

At least for now, we know what we don't know, Paul thought as the meeting adjourned.

Summary

There's no question—selling in the B2B world is complicated. And it is only getting more challenging, especially if you keep selling the way you always have. Aside from cost and other typical deal metrics, your customers also feel that complexity as uncertainty and risk. So why make it *harder* for them to choose you?

Yet that is what so many buyers tell me is happening. They either (1) don't understand your value proposition, (2) your proposal or offer does not easily link to the outcomes they want to achieve, (3) you are not prepared to negotiate effectively, or (4) they don't understand your past value delivered.

And it's often some—if not all—of the above.

Now here's some good news: Your customers have

unprecedented access to information about you, your business, your offerings, and other customers that are using your solutions. How is this good? As a salesperson, you're no longer a "two-legged sales brochure," and you can focus on more high-value activities. But the one thing your customer can never Google—and the most important step in their decision process—is determining which supplier knows them the best. Who understands the problems they are trying to solve or opportunities they are trying to seize? Who understands the outcomes they want to achieve and how they'll measure success?

Remember that customers buy outcomes, but we do not sell outcomes. Rather we *sell to* those outcomes. That means we must determine the right products and services (deal levers) that will produce those outcomes. So it's key that we determine early in the sales cycle what a great deal looks like for us *and the customer*—one that allows both parties to ultimately deliver the promised value.

The next book in this series, *The Irresistible Value Proposition*, picks up where this one leaves off. Would you like to know how Paul and his team develop an irresistible value proposition, one that will get the attention of the right people at MFS, make them want what Agile is selling and want it quickly? How will they navigate political land mines and deal with potentially hostile members of the steering committee?

Stay tuned!

> My goal with this book is to show the ways that we, as sellers, can make it challenging to award us must-win deals—then to reveal pragmatic ways to remove those challenges. It's simple, really. We just need to start with the outcomes that are important to the customer, then give them a clear way to understand how their outcomes directly align with our various products and services. In the next books in the series, we focus on the value proposition and clearly show how our value is better than the customer's alternative. We then present that value in a compelling proposal, then negotiate based on the customer's outcomes. After winning the deal, we articulate the value we've delivered as a foundation for building a stronger, sustainable business relationship that is good for both companies. As I've observed time and again, it's all about prioritizing *how* we sell over *what* we sell and creating real job security (for ourselves) in the process. Building trust and credibility through our selling approach makes it easy for our customers to choose us—and know that they have made the right choice.

I have created a generic "Deal Levers Thought Starter" tool (see the Appendix) that you can use when beginning to determine what a great deal may look like for a given opportunity. While the items in this version are applicable to most B2B businesses, it is by no means complete, but it should give you a good place to start. Every business and industry has its own proprietary language and items, so you'll want to "fill in the blanks" and customize it for your needs.

You can also download an electronic copy of the "Great Deal Thought Starter" from www.valuelifecycle.com.

While there, you may want to check out some of the videos that delve into the topics in this book. How's that for value?

Good Selling!

Steve

DEAL LEVERS – EXAMPLES

Converting Outcomes Into Key Elements of a Deal

1 Solution Levers

- Product #1
- Product #2
- Service #1
- Service #2
- Etc.

2 Contractual Levers

Which Contract

- Master Agreement
- Addendum
- SOW
- Purchase Agreement

Key Contract Terms

- Liability & Indemnification
- Service Level Agreements (SLA)
- Warranties
- Guarantees
- Cancellation Provisions

3 Business Transaction Levers

- Discount
- Volume
- Future Price Increases
- Date of Close
- Schedule / Completion Dates
- Contract Term
- Payment Terms
- Level of Support
- Training
- Travel Expenses

4 Strategic Levers

- Reference Account
- Co-Publish and Present Papers
- Joint Engagement Planning
- Customer Value Reviews (Who and When)
- Influence Technology Roadmap
- Introduction to Other Departments / Divisions

About the Author

 **STEVE THOMPSON** is the founder of Value Lifecycle™, which helps companies position, propose, negotiate, and close critical deals. In the past twenty years, he has worked on more than $15 billion in B2B deals in over a hundred different industries and twenty-four countries—for both selling and buying clients. Steve previously worked in operations, sales, and executive management at Westinghouse, Black & Decker, and DuPont. He served as a Nuclear Submarine Officer in the U.S. Navy.

49660780R00064

Made in the USA
Columbia, SC
25 January 2019